"Exceptional guidebook to
your self-discovery"

Life Coaching Workbook

By Petra Oblak

Life Coach, Entrepreneur & Philanthropist

Life Coaching Workbook

Discover yourself with this essential workbook

which will help you

on your life changing

journey.

You already have all the answers.

This workbook will enable you
to coach yourself.

This Life Coaching Workbook
is dedicated to everyone
who has throughout my life
brought tears of joy or tears of sadness
into my eyes.

It was both the joy and the sorrow
that encouraged me to take on the journey
of self-discovery,
unlocking the doors to my dreams and to
my true happiness.

Coaching Chapters:

1. Positive Thinking
2. Values and Beliefs
3. Reality and Overcoming Challenges
4. My Goals
5. My Options & Opportunities
6. My Journey Objectives
7. Cycle of Change
8. Motivation and Inspiration
9. Scoring System

Foreword

Congratulations!

You have just taken the very first step, step towards the change and towards taking the charge of your life. Taking this Life Coaching Workbook in your hands is your first step towards the understanding of your needs, your true values, your beliefs, and your true self.

This Life Coaching Workbook will help you to discover and awaken the true meaning of your life and your dreams. You can use this life coaching workbook to help you understand who you are and who you want to become. What are you desires in life, and how to achieve them.

This is your personal discovery book, your commitment plan, your examination check book and your planer. This workbook is your daily companion that will guide you and support you on your life-changing journey. This workbook is your friend you can trust with anything and everything.

This is your new begging.

This life coaching workbook will guide you step by step toward your desired goal. The complete book is based on self-discovery; it is your personal diary. Everything you write in this book, will come from your heart, therefore will be your desires, your plans and your goals. Nobody else's, just your dreams and this is why they are special and also achievable.

Life Coaching Chapters in this book cover all aspects of self-discovery and will help you to plan your life journey. Each section includes number of life coaching activities with empowering questions which will help you awaken your true self. You will coach yourself, you will be your own coach, coach you can trust.

The life coaching activities in this book will help you to understand your current life, help you to overcome challenges, set goals, and help you to discover what opportunities life already offers you, and what opportunities are awaiting for you.

In Journey Objectives and the Cycle of Change sections will help you understand your life changes and your life objectives. The last section will add Inspiration and Motivation to your life-changing journey.

This Life Coachi.ng Workbook can be used on its own or in addition to any life coaching session with a qualified Life Coach. Look out for coaching events, group coaching session or to book 1-1 coaching session at my website www.bestcoach.tv.

If you wish to go through the complete life coaching process, simply follow the workbook from the beginning to the end.

However, If you wish to work on a specific area of your life, that is absolutely fine. Maybe there is just one part of your life that needs attention–please trust yourself and go with any section from this workbook that you feel meets your need.

Maybe you need to work only on your positive beliefs and positive affirmations; maybe you've already set your goal but just need to work on small journey goals. Maybe you need to make your goal setting journey more fun and enjoyable. Whatever support and guidance you need, you will find it in this life coaching workbook.

The questions in this workbook are designed to help you examine your life, find the areas in your life that need improvement, and help you find your goal and commit to an action plan.

You can come back to this life coaching workbook at any time of your life. The beauty of this program is that you can work through it at your own pace and leisure.

Most importantly, enjoy the process of self discovery, enjoy the process of planning your life and enjoy living the life you have chosen to live.

Kindly Supporting you,

Petra, your Life Coach

Life

As Life whispers through our hearts,
awakening the force,
creating our existence,
there is only one intention.

The intention of peace and love
imbedded in our hearts
for us to feel
for us to live.

There is no grief or pain planed for us at
the point of creation.

We are given the freedom of choice,
the freedom of will.

Let us use it wisely
and
let us use it now.

Peace and love is real.

Chapter 1

Positive Thinking

There are many factors to happy and successful life, but the key to happy and fulfil life is positive thinking.

This is just a very short, basic, but factual statement about positive thinking. I will not go into depth on this subject, but wanted to touch base just enough for you to appreciate the great importance of keeping positive.

Keeping positive will help your motivation. Keeping a positive attitude will move you closer to your goal.

Facts:

Positive thinking helps your brain to produce the chemicals that give you a feeling of happiness. This chemical is called serotonin. Serotonin is chemical hormone that will give your body a feeling of happiness. By feeling happy your positive thoughts will continue.

On the other hand, if your thoughts are negative, the brain cells trigger the release of chemical called cortisone. Cortisone will give your body a feeling of great sadness, anger, and depression

With more negative thoughts, you get more chemical hormone cortisone, which produces more negative feelings.

During this state you are blocking the free flow of thoughts and ideas. It is not possible to set goals, make plans, or commit to action if you are feeling depressed; that is, if you are having negative thoughts.

Positive thoughts, positive affirmations, and empowering beliefs are the key to your life-changing journey. It all starts with positive attitude.

It is very important to keep positive when things are not going according to our plan. At times in our life, when we come across barriers and obstacles, it is even more important to keep our attitude positive. During challenging times, we must keep reminding ourselves of importance of keeping positive. Positive outlook will help and support us to overcome our challenges faster. There are tools in this workbook that will help you keep positive.

The biggest mistake, and one we all make at times, is when problems enter our life, we panic. We start thinking negatively, which brings on fear, and in this panic state it is hard to maintain a clear and focused mind.

Negative thinking will only pull us backward. We can only move forward, achieve things in our life and reach our dreams with positive attitude.

It is what you think about most of the time that creates your personality and your character. And it is your personality and your character that creates your life.

Watch your thoughts,
They become words
Watch your words,
They become actions
Watch your actions,
They become habits
Watch your habits,
They become your character
Watch your character,
It becomes your destiny.

-Ghandi

Chapter 2

Values and Beliefs

Before making changes in your life, before setting your goals and before making big decisions, **you need to get to know yourself.** Knowing yourself is crucial. Knowing yourself will ensure you will make the changes that are right for YOU and set the goals YOU want to ensure you get the life that YOU deserve.

Sometimes we set goals and make plans without taking into consideration our values. Goals and plans that are set against our values, will not make us happy and most likely, we will never reach them.

This is why the values are addressed in the first section of your life coaching workbook. This will give you the chance to get to know yourself. Take time to reflect on what is really important to you in your life. Take time to find out if you are neglecting some of your values in your life. If you are very unhappy and your life is in a state of emotional distress, ***evaluate your values.***

Once you establish what your core values are, once you know what these values mean to you, take an honest look at your life and ask yourself the following question:

1. Does my life truly represent my values?

2. Am I authentic and true to myself?

3. What in my life is not in line with my values?

4. What can I do to bring values back into my life?

For some people the issue of value will be more sensitive than for others.

If your values are part of your life, you will spend less time working on this. However, if you have abandoned some of your values during your life journey, you will want to revisit this section more often over the set period of time. You might want to dedicate more time during your life coaching program to work on your values and your beliefs.

You might want to come back to values when you set yourself your goals, just to ensure your goals are set within your morals, ethics, and principles. Then you will be more confident in setting your goal.

Too often in our life our focus is on other people. In my life-changing program I encourage you to focus on yourself, spend time planning your life. You should live your life the way you want, and you should ensure you live your life to your full potential—in the comfort of your values!

This workbook should become your daily companion. You will follow the coaching guidance to create the changes in your life, the changes needed to create your perfect life.

This workbook can also be used as a tool to help you overcome challenges of a particular project , issue or one area of your life that needs improving.

This Coaching Workbook will help you to create the life that you desire and deserve.

This workbook is your manual; relax and take time to write your answers. Some people find useful to mediate before they start working through the coaching manual or before starting the coaching session.

Always remember to live by your values.

Our values change through our life,
yet some values we hold deep in our hearts forever,
these are our ***core values.***

To live our lives against our values is the highest price we can pay in our life.

Our life is a reflection of our values.

My core values are *<u>(circle or write your own):</u>*

Achievement – Success – Stability – Status - Beauty Fame – Cooperation – Risk Taking – Teamwork Giving - Personality – Relationships – Religion Freedom - Responsibility – Reward – Security Self-respect - Serenity – Challenge – Children Success – Time - Truth – Wisdom – Socializing Charity – Tradition- Spirituality – Helping Teaching – Health – Sincerity - Responsibility Honesty – Trust – Soul – Connection - Career Personal Growth - Independence – Family Friendships – Faith – Compassion – Knowledge Fun Learning – Love – Loyalty – Money – Nature Pleasure - Power – Adventure – Security Recognition – Hard Work – Balance – Challenge Effectiveness - Understanding – Spontaneity Patience - Openness - Discipline – Peace - Awareness – Harmony

____

____

I regret many things, but I have never regretted the actions that originated from and within my values.

<u>What are your core values?</u>

Write your values that you have selected
in order of priority.

Which value is your core value?

You cannot afford to set goals and commit to actions without carefully considering your core values.

My values in the order of priority are:

1. ______________________________________

2. ______________________________________

3. ______________________________________

4. ______________________________________

5. ______________________________________

6. ______________________________________

7. ______________________________________

My values are the key to my true and lasting happiness.

<u>What do your values mean to you?</u>

What does each value that you selected mean to you?

What does the value represent?

The meaning of my values:

1. ____

2. ____

3. ____

4. ____

5. ____

6. ____

7. ____

My values are the key
to my true and lasting happiness.

Power of belief is what makes
or breaks our dreams.

You can have all the other elements required for success, but without a belief that you can and will succeed, you are blocking your own road to success. Only one thing is worse than not believing in yourself, and that is having a negative belief about yourself or your abilities.

We all have doubts, we all have negative beliefs, and we all get negative thoughts – sometimes. However, it's important for us to understand the power of negative beliefs, how to recognize them and how to change them to positive thoughts and to empowering beliefs.

We must recognize the damage negative beliefs are causing us and the anxiety and drama they create in our lives. We will learn to feel the benefits of positive affirmations, positive thoughts and the great effect they have on our life.

As you work through your life coaching workbook, especially thought the next section, you will learn a great deal about the way you think and how your thoughts affect your life. This part of the life coaching process is very sensitive. Be prepared to deal with your emotions as you go deeper into discovery of your beliefs. It will be painful at times.

You might recognize that you adopted some of your negative beliefs from your parents, friends, and family. Some negative beliefs are routed all the way back into your childhood. Some negative beliefs you adopted from people you love, people who are closest to your heart, people you trust. Recognition of these may be excruciating. Recognizing and dealing with negative beliefs might be painful and emotions will surface, but once they do, they will give you the chance to heal. You will learn how to change your negative beliefs into positive. You will discover how wonderful life is when your attitude toward yourself, your life, and life in general is positive. You will enjoy the feeling of being kind to yourself.

Elements in this section are excellent contributions to help you on your life-changing journey, which starts with being positive, having a great positive attitude, and having beliefs that will encouraging and motivate you.

Whatever you desire in your life, it all begins with having the right attitude and positive belief. Your life might be very challenging and full of difficulties at this very moment, but changes are possible, and they will start with having the right attitude and positive belief.

Therefore, before you set yourself a goal, before you start making the changes, before making big decisions, equip yourself with the right attitude, positive thoughts, and empowering beliefs. Your attitude will determine the level of your success and the extent of your happiness.

If you are holding on to negative beliefs, I encourage you to work on all elements provided in this section. Take time – as long as you need. Be thorough and pedantic. Don't leave any negative belief unturned and transformed all your negative belief into positives. Please remind yourself constantly. Write your positive affirmations and positive beliefs on notes or small cards and post them on your mirrors, kitchen cabinets, the fridge... write them on you hand, set reminders on your phone, in the calendar, wherever they will have ability of constant reminder.

We hold on to some negative beliefs from childhood, sometimes for years, sometimes the lifetime. Imagine hearing negative beliefs or repeating them to ourselves for years, imagine what this can do to your wellbeing.

It will take more than just ten minutes of your time to write them in your book. It will take time and commitment; therefore, constant reminders and constant attentions are required. But you will experience immense enjoyment when you recognize and abandon your negative beliefs and you will see the benefits that positive outlook will bring to your daily life.

What are our beliefs?

Beliefs are stories we no longer question.
We believe our stories to be true.

Most of the time, they are not even our beliefs; they are beliefs we have picked up from our family, friends, and colleagues.
And over the years, we have adopted them as our beliefs.

Beliefs are stories we perceive as reality. Stories about ourselves, our abilities, skills, looks,

BELIEFS will empower us to succeed or empower us to fail.

My negative beliefs are (write your own):

1. ____

2. ____

3. ____

4. ____

5. ____

6. ____

7. ____

LIFE happens to me in the light of my beliefs.

Where do your beliefs come from?

How long have you had these beliefs?
Do you remember them from childhood?
Who was saying these negative statements to you?
Did you hear these negative statements and adopt them as your own?
Did you only recently start to think negatively?
What triggered your negative thoughts

Where do my negative beliefs come from?

____

____

____

____

____

____

____

You don't need to believe in a higher power, just believe in yourself, and a higher power will follow.

When you think negative thoughts, you feel depressed and sad. When you feel depressed or sad, you can't take any positive actions or move forward.

When you think positive thoughts, you feel uplifted, empowered, and full of energy. You are motivated to do things in life.

You can choose the way you feel,

you can choose your thoughts.

Make your choice.

What am I feeling when I am thinking my NEGATIVE beliefs?

____

____

____

____

What am I feeling when I am thinking my POSITIVE beliefs?

____

____

____

____

Change your negative beliefs!

Have you decided to eliminate your negative thoughts from your daily life?

Negative thoughts are stubborn—they sneak up on us. Be aware and as soon as they surface, replace them with an empowering phrase.

You will soon see and feel benefits from positive thinking.

I know you are already feeling different,
just by being aware.
I hold on to only my empowering beliefs
(change your negative beliefs into positive ones):

1. ____

2. ____

3. ____

4. ____

5. ____

6. ____

7. ____

Positive Affirmations

Everything begins with the thought. So, the first step in your life-changing process is to act on your thoughts. Change your thoughts, and positive changes will start happening in your life.
Positive affirmations will change the way you think, talk, and act.

I choose to think wonderful thoughts.

Example (changing negative thought into positive affirmation)

"I feel stupid and will never get a good job".
"I am smart and I am getting a good job".

"I am fat and no one likes me".
"I am my perfect dress size and I am likeable".

My daily affirmations:

____

____

____

____

____

____

____

____

____

____

____

I am what I think I am; I feel how I want to feel.

If you have difficulty giving up negative thoughts, think what they are costing you right now! How are they affecting your life?

____

____

____

____

____

____

____

How will negative beliefs affect your life in the long term? If you continue with negative thoughts, what will your life be in five years?

____

____

____

____

____

____

____

What areas of my life are affected by my negative beliefs? What is happening to me and to my life because of my negative beliefs?

How will my life change for the better once I start to change my negative beliefs?

You know your positive beliefs now. Are people around you positive? If not, what can you do?

____

____

____

____

____

____

How do people around you contribute to your positive beliefs or your negative beliefs?

____

____

____

____

____

____

It is essential that you be surrounded by people who think positively and have a positive outlook on life.

You know your values now.
Do people around you share the same values?
If not, what can you do? What will you do?

____

____

____

____

____

____

How do people around you contribute to your values?

____

____

____

____

____

____

It is essential that you be surrounded by people who share your values.

Positive beliefs about myself:

____

____

____

____

____

____

____

I am remembering my values every day:

____

____

____

____

____

____

____

____

My daily positive affirmations:

____

____

____

____

____

____

____

____

I am:

Beautiful - Adventurous - Gorgeous - Lovely Positive - Responsible - Wise - Awesome - Confident – Caring - Intelligent - Noticeable Helpful - Funny - Independent - Giving - Special Determined – Committed – Authentic - Loving Playful - Healthy - Strong - Compassionate Successful – Hard Working – Considerate - Brave Loyal - Clever – Vigorous – The Best - Lovable Attractive – Understanding - Forgiving - Kind Friendly - Devoted - Happy - Attractive

____

____

____

____

____

____

____

____

I am what I say and what I do.

There is no such thing as absolute value in this world.
You can only estimate what a thing is worth to you.
-Charles Dudley Warner

Too many people today know the price of everything
and the value of nothing.
- Ann Landers

Example Affirmations:

I am in control of my thoughts.

I feel positive about my future.

I am able to take my steps towards my new life

My life is getting better every day.

My choices in life are in line with my values.

I am smart. I am beautiful. I am loved.

I feel good about myself and my future.

People in my life are kind with their words and their actions.

Chapter 3

Reality and Overcoming Challenges

There are things we can control in our life and therefore we can change them, but there are also things in our life that we cannot control or change.

We cannot escape problems, illnesses, aging, issues, suffering, death; but we can change the way we feel about them, we can change our attitudes toward them; we can call them our challenges and our stepping stones toward our growth. We get to decide how we feel about our "problems", we get to change them into "experiences" and "lessons". We can always turn them into something more positive, something that we can manage.

In order to change our life for the better we must first examine the reality of our daily life. What is our life really like? What challenges are we facing? By analyzing our life, we can take a control over it and make a plan to change it. By recognizing, seeing our problems for what they are, we can decide what to do about them, how to resolve them.

Taking responsibility for our lives is the first step toward change.

Though we have to look at our problems and challenges, we must not forget to examine our lives from positive point of view. We have to count our blessings too. Sometimes our lives are great, full of love and happiness, but we focus on this one problem that we have; all we see, talk about, and focus on is this one problem. It makes us feel our lives are falling apart, we forget to notice all the great deeds in our lives.

We have to be fair and look at our lives and at ourselves objectively.

Once we establish the true reality of our lives, we can start making changes. Only then we will know what is missing from our lives and what needs to change in order for our lives to improve. We don't want to change the things that work well, but we do want to change what needs to change!

As with all other sections in this workbook, the same rule applies in this section. Please be honest. Remember, this is your life coaching workbook, your commitment book, your examination book that will help you transform your life. Reflect on your life honestly. If you are to establish your goal and to ensure you reach your dreams, we must know where you are today. We must know what is good in your life, we must know what needs to be removed from your life and we need to know what will continue in your life to ensure your happiness and your well-being.

In order to make changes, we must know what needs to change. We do not want to make changes that we might regret later. We do not want to make decisions that we might regret later. This is why this section is extremely important.

Recognizing the size of the problem is also important. You may look closer to your problem and realize it is not such a big deal after all. By analyzing your problems, you will find the solutions. By being aware of your obstacles, you will know how to recognize them and avoid them today and in the future.

In our lives we try to ignore obstacles and problems; we just don't want to deal with them. I encourage you to DEAL with them today. To know yourself and you know your life; you must recognize all that life gives you, good and bad, both are necessary for your growth and your life-changing journey.

If you need help to relax before or while you participate in this section of your book, perhaps spend some time meditating, listening to music, relaxing or taking a walk; whatever helps you to put your mind at ease.

What needs to change in your life?

Unless something changes, the life you live today is the life you will live tomorrow.

If you are not happy with your life, start analysing it now.

Be honest to yourself and admit if there is problem in your life.

Don't judge yourself.

Look at the reality of your life;
look for anything that is blocking your happiness or stopping you from changing it for better.

Reflect on where you are today, what you're your stepping stones in your life so far.

Remember; you are the force that can and will change your life for better.

What is going on right now in my life that tells me

that I have a problem?

____

____

____

____

____

____

____

What is missing from my life?

____

____

____

____

____

____

____

What is good in your life?

You need to know what is missing in your life;
too often we focus on what we don't have,
rather than on what we do have in our life.

We mustn't be too hard on ourselves.

We find it hard to acknowledge our successes,
our breakthroughs, and our good deeds.

Sometime we work so hard to reach our goals that once we achieve them, we often focus only on a difficult journey we had, rather than on great results.

It is time to look at everything that is good in our lives.
Things, people, moments, and events
that make us happy.

Let acknowledgment of your blessings become part of your daily routine.

What is happening in my life that is good and that I want it to stay in my life?

____

____

____

____

____

____

____

What things have I done so far to improve my life?

____

____

____

____

____

____

____

Good things happen to me every day!

What possible obstacles are in your way that could prevent you from moving forward?

Obstacles and barriers will always exist.

Make them your friends, not your enemies.

You need them throughout your life.
They act as checkpoints on your life journey.

Life will never create the obstacles
that you cannot overcome.

Your experiences come from overcoming your obstacles,
and it is experience that will guide you when you make your next choice.

I know these obstacles will prevent me from moving forward. Obstacles that I can identify:

____

____

____

____

____

____

____

____

____

____

____

____

My obstacles are really just challenges that help me make better choices and encourage me to introduce positive changes into my life.

What can you do to overcome your current obstacles?

Sometimes we focus mainly on the problem and the situation that the problem is creating.

Let us better focus on finding a solution
to our problems.

What can I do to overcome my challenges?

____

____

____

____

____

____

____

Do I need to ask for help or advice?
If so, who can I ask for help or for advice?

____

____

____

____

____

____

____

____

Every problem is as big as we make it to be.

Will I need to change to overcome my challenges?

Our thoughts create our reality and our behaviour determines who we are and what we do.

Sometimes the challenges are set to be one size too big, so that we need to grow by changing our thinking or our behaviour in order to be strong enough to handle them.

My thoughts that will need to change:

____

____

____

____

____

My behaviour that will need to change:

____

____

____

____

____

Change is part of my life;
I change for the better with ease and grace.

Taking control

I am sorry that I have to confront you with this issue, but it is important.
Are you in control?

When we face problems and challenges, too often we blame others for our misfortune.
This is about discovery, this is about you taking control of your life, by starting to take responsibility for your challenges.

Whom do I blame for my problems, obstacles, and issues in my life?

____

____

____

____

I intend to stop blaming; myself or others, or situations. From now on, I will:

____

____

____

____

There is no need for blaming, things happen for a reason. I have the power, courage, and faith to take full responsibility of my life and make changes.

<u>My life without problems and obstacles?</u>

Relax and think as far back as you can remember revisit your childhood, your teenage years, your early adulthood, your life. Remember the three most challenging situations from your life:

____

____

____

What did you do to overcome them?

____

____

____

____

____

How did your life change afterwards?

____

____

____

____

How do you feel about these past challenges now?

____

____

____

____

____

____

____

I am a survivor of my life challenges and I always move on with my head held high!

What difficulties in life did my parents or grandparents have to face?

____

____

____

____

____

____

How did their challenges and difficulties affect my experience growing up and my life as a whole?

____

____

____

____

____

____

I understand that my parents did their best according to their knowledge and their abilities.
I do the same.

What would my life be like so far if I had no challenges on the way to make me stronger?

____

____

____

____

____

____

What is this telling me? What am I learning from my answers?

____

____

____

____

____

____

If you had a magic wand and you could make one of your problems / challenges / issues disappear, which one would it be?

____

This is the biggest issue/problem in your life.

What can you do to resolve this issue?

____

____

____

____

What will you do to resolve this issue?

____

____

____

____

How will your life change once this issue is resolved?

____

____

____

____

Select one of your problems. Think about it as ridiculous. Make fun out of it. See the funny side of it.

____

____

____

____

____

Is there is a person in your life that makes your life difficult, makes you suffer? Think about her or him in a ridiculous situation. Ridicule him /her:

____

____

____

____

____

____

I can chouse to laugh at my problems...

On regular basis, visualize and see your problem resolved, visualize yourself overcoming your challenges.

What do you see when you see your problem resolved? How do you feel?

____

____

____

____

____

____

See yourself without a problem, without an issue, without stress.

What does your life look like when your problem has dissolved?

____

____

____

____

____

____

Draw the picture of your problem being resolved: (or create a collage)

Revisit this picture regularly.

Stand alone activity: (can be used with any subject)
A different perspective will show you the problem from a different angle.

Who is your favourite sports figure?

____

____

What daily challenges does he or she face?

____

____

How do you think he or she deals with challenges?

____

____

How do you think he or she would deal with your challenges?

____

____

____

____

How can you use these answers to help you with you challenges?

I might be able to deal with the problem more easily from a different perspective.

Should have only six months to live, what challenges would you consider your main problems?

____

____

____

____

____

How would you deal with them differently?

____

____

____

____

____

____

Knowing is not enough; we must apply. Willing is not enough; we must DO.

-Johann Wolfgang von Goethe

Chapter 4

My GOALS

Until now we were examining our lives and getting to know ourselves. We were evaluating our belief systems, our values, and our realities and existence that make up the hours in our days. Doing so we have shaken our beliefs and our existence, our emotions surfaced, but we have given ourselves a chance to wake up from our delusions of unhappy lives. We are ready to start making positive changes in our lives, to take charge, to commit.

With changing our beliefs, our lives should by now be more positive. We should by now be looking at what is good in our lives and how we can make it even better. We have removed everything that no longer serves our purposes in our lives, and we have removed everything that could stop us moving forward toward our dreams, and we disconnected from people or situations that made our lives gloomy. If we did not remove everything, at least I am sure we started the process in some way.
We must accept, that sometimes, and some issues are part of on-going self-development.

But it is time to start setting our goals. Now is a good time to start dreaming again, making plans, and setting goals.

Having a goal in your life will give you motivation and meaning. You will know where you want to go in your life and what you want to achieve. Setting goals will help you to looking forward in life, rather than focus on the past.

By setting goals, you are taking charge of your life. You are the one deciding how to live your life. This feels great. We all have dreams, but not everyone is willing to act on them. The secret path to your dreams leads through your goals. You set the goals and commit to action and, before you know it, you will be live your dreams.

You should always have long-term goals or, as I call them, your life goals. These are goals that take time and commitment and require years, decades, or a lifetime to achieve. However, remember, the journey itself toward those goals is your life that you live, day after day.

Short-time goals to achieve different things in life are important to keep us focused and on track. Keep revising both goals and actions daily.

Enjoy setting your goals and enjoy the journey toward your better, more fulfilling life.

When you attend to your goals daily, you will see the progress faster than you can imagine. When you make one step, one action—no matter how small—every day, it all amounts to a greater life and greater you.

Life is chain of events, so why not choose the events that you wish to see in your life, rather than bouncing from one to the other without having your own choice.

Your life is reflection of you; your thoughts and your actions. And you decide what thoughts you think and what actions you take.

Again, if you have difficulty dreaming, visualising, or setting goals, please take some time for life coaching meditation that will help you relax. These meditations are helpful at any time. You can reserve some time during the day for your contemplation time, or just before you start to work on this book. You can also listen or watch life coaching meditation when you write and make notes in your life coaching workbook.

Enjoy!

What is the force behind my goal?

We set goals because we want to change and because we want to change our lives for better.

What is the force behind your goal? What is pushing you, guiding you, or encouraging you to make changes and to reach your goals?

I am reaching my goals because of the force that is empowering me:

____

____

____

____

____

____

____

____

I move towards my goal, rather than away from something I don't like. I am always moving forward... I focus on the future.

Love and optimism are forces that guide me toward my goal.

<u>List the areas of your life, topic or issue that needs improving;</u>

There are many areas of our lives, and each area will include different issues and projects.
I encourage you to examine your complete life, all areas, topics, projects, people in your life—everything. Put your life under microscope.

What part of your life needs to improve?

Areas and topics of my life that need attention/improvement:

1.____________________________________

2.

____

3.

____

4.____________________________________

5.___________________________________

6.___________________________________

7. ___________________________________

I recognize what needs to change in my life.

I take control of my life before it has a chance to take control of me.

What is your goal?

It is time to write down your goal. This goal will help you change the areas of your life you selected that needs improving.

Make your goal setting FUN.
What exactly do you want?

Be specific:

Remember that the goal must be your own goal, not someone else's. The goal must be positive, realistic, possible to achieve, but at the same challenging, and written in the present tense.
Your goal must be LEGAL!

You should write a goal for each area that needs improving.

Example:

The area of my life that needs to improve is my health. My Goal is: ***Get fit***

My job is very stressful, it effects my life badly.
My goal: ***I am getting a new Job***

Select the area/issue (in the order of importance / priority) from the list above and write a **GOAL** for each (goal that once achieved will resolve your issue or improve your area of concern):

1.______________________________________

2. ______________________________________

3.______________________________________

4.______________________________________

5.______________________________________

6.______________________________________

7. ______________________________________

Now, on the line next to the goal (above) write the deadline - by which date you want to achieve this goal. Make it realistic!

I have always wanted to change my life. I always wanted to reach these goals.

Now I don't just "want" it–I decided to have it / to do it.

What will happen when you reach your goal?

When setting a goal, think about what you will **be**, what you will be **doing** and what you will **have** when you reach your goal!
Who will you be with?

What will I **be** when I reach my goal?

____

____

____

____

What will I be **doing** when I reach my goal?

____

____

____

____

What will I **have** when I reach my goal?

____

____

____

____

Who will I be with?

____

____

____

____

What can stop me reaching my goal?

Ask yourself the following questions:

Do I have time to reach my goals? If not, what can I do to make time?

____

____

How can I better organize myself?

____

____

____

____

____

____

____

Is there anything that I need to remove from my life?

____

____

____

____

____

____

____

____

Do I have the motivation?

____

____

____

____

____

____

____

How can I increase my energies and my motivation?

____

____

____

____

____

____

____

____

Do I need / have financial support? If not what can I do about it?

____

____

____

____

____

____

____

Do I surround myself with people who support me? If not, what can I do about it?

____

____

____

____

____

____

____

____

What can come between me and my goal?

____

____

____

____

____

____

____

____

What can stop me achieving my goal?

____

____

____

____

____

____

____

____

What can I do to remove these obstacles?

____

____

____

____

____

____

____

____

Your goals at a glance

Answer the following questions with yes or no. (You will find a scoring system at the end of the book that will help you understand the score.)

1. Is my goal personal? Is it what "I" want?

____

2. Do I have the support I need?

____

3. Did I set a realistic time scale?

____

4. Did I take a positive approach?

____

5. Do I have the skills and knowledge to reach my goal? If not, what will I do about it?

____

6. Does my goal fit my purpose and the meaning of my life?

____

7. Do I believe I can reach my goal?

____

8. Is my goal in line with my values?

____

9. Will my goal contribute to my happiness?

____

10. On a scale of 1-7, how committed am I to reach my goal?

____

Personal Notes:

____

____

____

____

____

____

____

____

____

____

____

____

____

____

If the answer to any of the questions is NO, what action can I take?

1.____________________________________

2.____________________________________

3.____________________________________

4.____________________________________

5.____________________________________

6.____________________________________

7. ____________________________________

My score is lower than 5.

What action will I take to increase my score?

____

____

____

____

I have examined and double-checked all my goals to ensure that I know what to do when barriers appear. I am confident.

Projects in my life that need attention:
(in order of priority)

The GOALS to make my projects happen:

My GOAL is:

1.____

My deadline: ______________________________

2.____

My deadline: ______________________________

3.____

My deadline: ______________________________

My first step/action I will take to make me closer to my goals:

1.____

When: ___________________________________

2.____

When: ___________________________________

3.____

When: ___________________________________

My other GOALS

MY GOAL IS:

____

____

____

What made me choose this goal:

____

____

____

____

5 things I like most about my goal:

____

____

____

____

____

____

When I come across challenges, I am prepared. I know what to do:

My possible challenges which may prevent me to reach my Goals:

____

____

____

____

____

____

How can I avoid the challenges?

____

____

____

____

____

____

MY BIG GOAL (something that you always wanted in your life, something you are super passionate about, something that makes your heart jump - something that you always thought was out of your reach

____

____

____

Small goals that I will have to get to

before I reach my big GOAL

___________________ ___________________

___________________ ___________________

___________________ ___________________

___________________ ___________________

___________________ ___________________

MY MAIN ACTIONs

Small actions I will have to
Undertake, before I can undertake
my main ACTION

Picture of my BIG Goal (or collage)

Date: _____________ Signature: _______________

Picture of me reaching my Goal: (or collage)

Date: _____________ Signature: ______________

My Childhood Dream

When I was a child, I had dreams.
I always wanted to be...do...or have...

____

____

____

____

____

____

What or who stopped me reaching my childhood dreams in the past:

____

____

____

____

____

____

Have the dream so big, that you cannot achieve it, until you grow into the person, who can.

-Unknown

Today I decide to act on my Childhood Dream

____

____

____

The actions I will take

______________________ ______________________

______________________ ______________________

______________________ ______________________

I will achieve my childhood dream

By this Date: ________________________________

The future belongs to those who believe in the beauty of their dreams.

-Eleanor Roosevelt

My Dreams further notes:

Chapter 5

My Options and Opportunities

The choices we make in our lives determine our destiny and our future. The choices we make fill our days with either joy or with sadness. The choices we make put smiles or tears on our faces.

What are the right and wrong choices?

Some people say there are no right or wrong choices. However, the right choices complete your life with happiness, and the wrong choices make you stressed and depressed, both have consequences.

So how can we to ensure that we make the right choices in our lives?

By taking into account everything we talked about until now. By taking into account everything you have written in your life coaching workbook so far. To take your feelings, your values, your beliefs and consider your options, evaluate your life, then you will have a chance to make the right choice that is right for you. Only you know what the right option for you is.

In this section we will be looking at the number of options that are available to you. We are investigating your opportunities. A vast number of options and opportunities are available to you at every moment of your life; you just need to take time to notice them.

Most of the time we say to ourselves; "I have no other option but to do...which is really not what I want, but I have no choice." OK, we cannot control everything that is going on around us, but we have always the right to do what we want.

When we are presented with the situation, when we need to choose, when we are looking for the best way to move forward, we must take time and brainstorm, write down as many options as possible, no matter how crazy, realistic or unrealistic they might sound.

Once you have shredded all the options in your life, no matter how wild, then you can evaluate them. What might sound crazy at the beginning might not sound as crazy once you think about it. Only when you take time to evaluate all of your options, only then do you have a chance to make the right decisions. Remembering at all times, that whatever we do, consequences will show up in our lives, so it is important to take make the right choices.

Opportunities are presented to us daily. We must be present in a moment to see them. Too often we are focused on our future or our past, so present moments and its opportunities are skipping by unnoticed. We have to be open-minded too. Too often we shut the door to our opportunities too soon. Sometimes we dismiss them before we even consider them properly.

Once you start your self-discovery journey, once you start taking charge of your life, life will present you with endless opportunities. Be on the lookout. When you set yourself goals and start making progress toward them, opportunities will be there for you.

Your life will present you with crossroads; think and evaluate each option before taking the ride.

The more time you devote to Opportunities and Options section, the better for you. Even when you can't think of anything else, when you feel there is no other opportunity or option available to you, try to discover one more. You never know, maybe that will be the life-changing one for you.

Follow your heart and your intuition; your heart will always know what is good for you. Your heart will never mislead you, ever.

Taking time and thoroughly considering all the options is the best way forward. Meditate, take walks, engage in sports, or read; all this will help you to draw closer to your right option.

Do not settle for one or two options that you might see immediately. Explore and find as many as you can. When you meditate on your options, new and unexpected potential will arise as you awaken your inner true feelings. Follow your heart when awaking your options and follow your heart when choosing the option.

Do not rush. Taking time to evaluate now will save you lots of stress or unhappiness in the future. Remember, the right decision now will lead you to new great opportunities, and they will lead you to even more such opportunities in life.

The wrong options will just lead to more wrong opportunities, it's a chain reaction.

If anything unexpected surfaces at this moment, please make a note of your thought. Any past experiences or past regrets?

Are you limiting yourself?

Sometimes we limit ourselves in our lives.
As if life wasn't challenging enough.
We limit our abilities, we limit our opportunities, and we limit our opportunities.
We limit our belief systems so our opportunities and options in life become limited.

I challenge you to recognize your own limitations, limitations you set by yourself.

Ask yourself the following questions:

Am I limiting myself in any way? What are things that I do or say to myself that limit my abilities to succeed?

____

____

____

____

____

I make my life easier by removing my own limitations.

If there were no consequences in your life, what would you do?

We desire something.
We dream about it, we talk about, we want it, but then we start to worry about it. And every possible negative outcome disturbs our minds.

What would DO in my life, if I could not fail?

____

____

____

____

____

____

I live my life to my full potential

Every day brings new opportunities into our lives, we just need to open our eyes.

As soon as we start thinking of changing, making choices, and setting goals, life itself will present opportunities and options.

You already have opportunities and options available to you, right now.

List of opportunities that already exist in my life:

____

____

____

____

____

____

____

____

____

New opportunities present themselves to me every day. I notice them and I act on them.

Do you need resources?

We all have the opportunities and options required to reach our goal. They are our direction signs and our helpers on the way.

But what resources or help will you need to take the right turns and stay on track?

What resources or help do I already have?

____

____

____

____

____

____

What other resources and help will I need?

____

____

____

____

____

____

Having Fun?

Take a look at your list of opportunities and options.

What are you feeling?

On a scale of 1-7, how is your:

Motivation and Enjoyment

Satisfaction on all levels

Select the option that feels right for you, taking into consideration your values and beliefs.

Feelings that surface when I think about my opportunities and my options:

____

____

____

____

____

____

____

I see myself having fun when I think about my opportunities and options.

Make your choice.

From the list of options that you created, write the options that are best suited to you.

Select the options and opportunities that feel right for you, taking in consideration everything we worked on so far.

From the endless list of my options that have presented themselves to me, I have selected the options I know will help me most to reach my goal:

____

____

____

____

____

____

The outcome of my life is the result of my choices

Can my selected options lead me to new opportunities?

Every time we make the first step, every time we act on our opportunity, new doors open for us to make our journey easier.

What new doors will your chosen options open for you?

Each new open door is a new opportunity that will open up new possibilities and will generate new goals.

The choices I make opens the doors to new opportunities; new opportunities generate new goals:

1.____________________________________

2. ____________________________________

3. ____________________________________

4.____________________________________

5. ____________________________________

6. ____________________________________

7. ____________________________________

My life is taking shape.

I am happy with the progress I am making.

If my life had endless opportunities, what would they be?

____

____

____

____

____

____

____

If my life had endless options, what would they be?

____

____

____

____

____

____

____

What opportunities did my parents have? (or my friends, my idol)

____

____

____

____

____

____

____

Which options did they take?

____

____

____

____

____

____

____

How different would their lives be if they had made different choices?

____

____

____

____

____

____

How different would my life be if my parents had made different choices?

____

____

____

____

____

____

____

____

How can new opportunities change my life?

My affirmations that will help me see new opportunities:

Did I ever miss a good opportunity in my life? What was it?

____

____

____

____

____

____

____

____

What did I learn from this experience?

____

____

____

____

____

____

____

What can I do to create more new opportunities?

____

____

____

____

____

____

____

____

How can I recognize a good opportunity?

____

____

____

____

____

____

____

____

What opportunities did I act on in my life that changed my life for the better?

How did my life change for the better?

If I had another chance, would I make a different decision today?

____

____

____

____

____

____

____

____

How would my life be different? Would it be better?

____

____

____

____

____

____

____

Relationship and Family

What opportunities and options do I have in my life to be happy in a relationship or enjoy a happy family life?

____

____

____

____

____

____

____

____

What will I do to act on my options and opportunities?

____

____

____

____

____

____

Health and Fitness

What opportunities and options do I have in my life to be fit and healthy?

____

____

____

____

____

____

____

____

What will I do to act on my options and opportunities?

____

____

____

____

____

____

Career

What opportunities and options do I have in my life to create success in my career?

____

____

____

____

____

____

____

____

What will I do to act on my options?

____

____

____

____

____

____

____

Interests and Hobbies

What opportunities and options do I have to create more fun and joy in my life?

____

____

____

____

____

____

____

____

What will I do to act on my options?

____

____

____

____

____

____

Further notes on options and opportunities in your life. How will you know when you make the right choice? Imagine what your life will look like in 5 years' time. Who will you be in 5 years time, who will you be with after making the decision for particular option.
What are people saying about you?

____

____

____

____

____

____

____

____

____

____

____

____

Chapter 6

My Journey Objectives

The aim of this life coaching workbook is to help you to continue your life-changing journey.

If you can commit to work on this life coaching workbook daily, if only for ten minutes during your coffee break, this attention will remind you of your objectives and your goals. By constant self-observation, you will continue on your self-development journey and you will see the progress, which will give you great confidence and motivation. Your life coaching workbook will help you to take that first step, the first step we all find most difficult to take.

Once you commit to the first step, once you take the first step, the rest of the journey will get easier. However, you will need to be focused daily and attend to your actions that you have carefully planned.

The best way to keep focused and determined is to write your goals and your action plans. Therefore, this commitment book is a great reminder for your life-changing journey. Keeping a journal will also help noticeably. Now that you have started your life-changing journey, you will be more aware of your life, your actions, and events happening in your life.

Recording the changes, challenges, successes, and seatbacks will help your motivation and will keep your journey in perspective. Always date the journals and notes you write in this workbook so that you can track your progress.

Scoring your commitment is essential. Please score your action commitment, your time scale commitment, and your goal commitment. Checking your commitment will show your devotion to your goal. Please refer to scoring system that is toward the end of this book.

Consistence is vital. Attending to your workbook will help you to be consistent and to continue working toward your goal, step by step. The workbook will remind you to evaluate your actions daily. These small daily steps and actions will make your dream come true. Without daily commitment and consistency, your goal will be keep slipping away from your reach.

Every goal that you set for yourself should be written down together with a commitment of the first step that you will take. Complete the action plan with times and dates to make your goals visible and reachable. By constantly revisiting your journey, you will also maintain your motivation and confidence, as you will be able to see your progress.

<u>Your journey toward your goal is your life</u>. The moments of the day create your life, so remember that the journey is as important as the goal itself. The journey toward your dream is as significant as your dream. The journey may last a long period of time, while the goal itself can be momentarily.

Each small goal on your way to your goal is as important as your end goal. Celebrate and enjoy each destination that you reach.

Commitment!

Today I am committing to take action.

I have dreamed; I had my thoughts; I have made decisions; I have evaluated my opportunities and I made my choice.

Today I am committing to act.

For my Goal: ________________________________

I am committing to take the following action or actions:

____

____

____

____

____

What are actions requiring of me to do?

____

____

____

____

My life will never be the same again
—that's a promise.

The first step that I will take:

A journey of one thousand miles begins with the first step.

Feel the excitement, accept the challenge.

Every step you take will generate great feelings of achievement and purpose.

My goal is: ___________________________________

I plan to reach my goal by: ____________________

The first step I will take toward this goal is:

____

____

I plan to take this first step (date): ______________

What do I need in order to take the first step:

____

____

____

____

____

How /where will I get it:

____

____

____

____

Commitment scale 1 - 2 - 3 - 4 - 5 - 6 - 7

<u>The first step that I will take:</u>

A journey of one thousand miles begins with the first step.

Feel the excitement, accept the challenge.

Every step you take will generate great feelings of achievement and purpose.

My goal is: __________________________________

I plan to reach my goal by: ____________________

The first step I will take toward this goal is:

____

____

I plan to take this first step (date): ______________

What do I need in order to take the first step:

____

____

____

____

____

How /where will I get it:

____

____

____

____

Commitment scale 1 – 2 – 3 – 4 – 5 – 6 – 7

The first step that I will take:

A journey of one thousand miles begins with the first step.

Feel the excitement, accept the challenge.

Every step you take will generate great feelings of achievement and purpose.

My goal is: ____________________________________

I plan to reach my goal by: ____________________

The first step I will take toward this goal is:

____

____

I plan to take this first step (date): ______________

What do I need in order to take the first step:

____

____

____

____

____

How /where will I get it:

____

____

____

____

Commitment scale 1 - 2 - 3 - 4 - 5 - 6 - 7

My Long-Term Plan

It might take months or years for some of our goals to manifest in our life.
It is essential that we have long-term goals.
These are our road map goals, as they will give us direction and keep us on track.

My Long-Term GOAL:

____

Actions I will take:	Date:
1. ____________________	________________
2. ____________________	________________
3. ____________________	________________
4. ____________________	________________
5. ____________________	________________
6. ____________________	________________
7. ____________________	________________

Commitment scale 1 – 2 – 3 – 4 – 5 – 6 – 7

As I write my goals and my action plan,
my dreams are manifesting in my life.

My Short-Term Plan

On a day-to-day basis you will focus on your short-term plan. These are actions you will take on a daily or weekly basis.
These consistent daily and weekly contributions will make the whole difference to your life. These daily and weekly actions are actions of change; these are creating your life, step by step, day by day.

My Short-Term GOAL:

Actions I will take: Date:

1. ____________________ ________________

2. ____________________ ________________

3. ____________________ ________________

4. ____________________ ________________

5. ____________________ ________________

6. ____________________ ________________

7. ____________________ ________________

Commitment scale 1 - 2 - 3 - 4 - 5 - 6 - 7

My days are filled with activities that I enjoy.

Every day I start with my goal in mind.

Every day you feel different.

Your energies are unique, you might meet new people, have new surroundings; your schedule will change. Plan and be prepared for your day's challenges. Start your day with your goal and your purpose in mind.

I am focused but flexible.

What am I particularly looking forward to doing today?

____

____

____

____

Things that may bring me stress and anxiety:

____

____

____

____

How can I avoid or limit the stress and anxiety? What can I do and will do to help me with the stress?

____

____

____

____

____

____

____

____

Are there any projects or issues that need addressing to prevent further stress?

____

____

____

____

____

____

Every night I revisit my progress.

Express gratitude for today.

If your day did not go according to your plan...
If you feel you failed in any way...
DO NOT JUDGE your actions, your behaviour, your thoughts or your words.
Just accept them as part of the process; acknowledge them and let them go.

They no longer serve your purpose.

What did I do well today?

____

____

____

____

____

What could I do differently today?

____

____

____

____

What will I do differently tomorrow?

____

____

____

____

____

What did I learn from today's life experience?

____

____

____

____

____

What do I want more of in my life?

____

____

____

____

Today I am grateful for:

People I am grateful for today:

My Goal:

____

Actions I will take:

____

____

____

By taking positive actions, my life will change for better. What will my life look like?

____

____

____

Once I achieve my goal, what will my life look like?

____

____

____

Commitment scale 1 - 2 - 3 - 4 - 5 - 6 - 7

With new goal comes new responsibility:

____

____

____

With new actions come new opportunities:

____

____

____

With new opportunities comes new life:

____

____

____

My life looks like this:

____

____

____

My Short-Term Goal

____

ACTIONS

Actions I will take:	On this Date:
1. ________________	______________
2. ________________	______________
3. ________________	______________
4. ________________	______________
5. ________________	______________
6. ________________	______________
7. ________________	______________

Commitment scale 1 - 2 - 3 - 4 - 5 - 6 - 7

My Long-Term Goal

____

ACTIONS

Actions I will take: On this Date:

1. ________________ ______________
2. ________________ ______________
3. ________________ ______________
4. ________________ ______________
5. ________________ ______________
6. ________________ ______________
7. ________________ ______________

Commitment scale 1 - 2 - 3 - 4 - 5 - 6 - 7

My GOAL is:

____

____

The first step I am taking to reach my goal:

____

____

My deadline:

____

____

The weekly steps I will take, staps that will bring me closer to my goal:

____

____

____

____

____

My positive affirmation:

____

Commitment scale 1 - 2 - 3 - 4 - 5 - 6 - 7

My GOAL is:

____

____

The first step I am taking to reach my goal:

____

____

My deadline:

____

____

The weekly steps I will take, staps that will bring me closer to my goal:

____

____

____

____

____

____

My positive affirmation:

____

Commitment scale 1 – 2 – 3 – 4 – 5 – 6 – 7

When I come across my challenges, I am prepared, and I know what to do.

Possible obstacles that may stop me from reaching my goal:

____

____

____

____

____

____

What can I do to prevent this from happening?

____

____

____

____

____

____

When I come across my challenges, I am prepared, and I know what to do.

Possible obstacles that may stop me from taking action:

____

____

____

____

____

What can I do to prevent this happening?

____

____

____

____

____

What can make my action plan more fun and motivating?

____

____

____

____

MY BIG GOAL

____

____

The small goals I will have to reach before I reach my big GOAL

______________________ ______________________

______________________ ______________________

______________________ ______________________

______________________ ______________________

Commitment scale 1 - 2 - 3 - 4 - 5 - 6 - 7

My ACTION plan:

The small actions I will have to take before I can take my big ACTION

Commitment scale 1 - 2 - 3 - 4 - 5 - 6 - 7

My old habits are preventing me to move forward. The habits that need to change are:

1. ___________________________________

2. ___________________________________

3. ___________________________________

4. ___________________________________

5. ___________________________________

Every day I focus on developing and maintaining new habits. I will change the above habits into new positive habits:

1. ___________________________________

2. ___________________________________

3. ___________________________________

4. ___________________________________

5. ___________________________________

My daily actions create my good habits.

I do my best to keep good habits in my life and to avoid getting involved in my old habits which prevent me from reaching my goals.

What do I need to do to avoid my old habits repeating; old habits which no longer serve my purpose?

1. ________________________________

2. ________________________________

3. ________________________________

4. ________________________________

5. ________________________________

I say **YES** to everything that takes me step closer to my goal, and **NO** to everything else.

In order to reach my goal, I am making the following changes in my daily life:

1. ________________________________

2. ________________________________

3. ________________________________

4. ________________________________

5. ________________________________

I enjoy making changes; they make my life interesting and on course.

Commitment scale 1 - 2 - 3 - 4 - 5 - 6 - 7

In order to reach my goal, I am making the right choices. When I find it difficult to resist my old habits, I remember the benefits my goal will bring.

1. ______________________________

2. ______________________________

3. ______________________________

4. ______________________________

5. ______________________________

People around me encourage my positive process of change.

Benefits my goals will bring to my life:

1. ______________________________

2. ______________________________

3. ______________________________

Actions I wish to take to make a small difference in the world.

I am blessed with courage, strength, willpower, health, and wealth.
I am grateful to the Creator for all these gifts.
I wish to express my gratitude by giving back small tokens of appreciation to those who are less fortunate.

I will contribute to the world and to people who are less fortunate, by taking the following steps/ actions:

____

____

____

____

How will others benefit from my actions?

____

____

____

____

Commitment scale 1 - 2 - 3 - 4 - 5 - 6 - 7

A goal is a dream with a deadline.

-Napoleon Hill

Never tell me the sky's the limit
When there are footprints on the moon.

-Unknown

The greater danger for most of us is
not that our aim is too high and we miss it,
but that it is too low and we hit it.

-Michelangelo

Goals that are not written down are just wishes.

-Unknown

My own quote:

____

____

Chapter 7

Cycle of Change

This is fun part of the life coaching workbook. I found the cycle of change amusing. Please take it lightly and have fun with it. When you learn how the cycle of change works, you will understand the process and you will be able to see why it is sometimes so difficult to change. You will also learn to read other people's changing patterns.

We all go through the cycle of change. This cycle applies to all areas of our lives, to all issues and situations. It applies to any change you are going through. It is important that you understand where you are in the cycle of change with your different goals, situations, life adjustments, or plans.

When you know where you are, you will be able to move forward, you will be able to recognize the challenges and you will be able to put preventions in place to ensure you are keep moving forward or continue maintaining your lifestyle.

This part of the workbook is specifically beneficial to those who like the things to stay as they are. This part of the workbook is for people who don't like changes. But sometimes the changes are inventible, therefore its easer to accept the change than try to stop it.

Life is ongoing, endless change.

Everything changes. We cannot stop the process of change; we must learn to accept the change and grow with it.

Life is simply too difficult and frustrating if we are going to work against the natural cycle of change.

You will also recognize that sometimes we run around in a circle from rejection to action, or from rejection to relapse.

We run around and every time we fail it takes extra energy to start the process of change again. It would be so much easier to stay in maintenance section, it would take so much less energy, and our motivation and our confidence would be at our highest level. We would feel great and we would have a feeling of accomplishment.

With constantly running in circles it's frustrating and we are in danger that one day it will end in rejection and we won't have sufficient energy to get up and climb the cycle of change again.

Therefore, do take time to understand how your cycle of change works in every area of your life and in every situation you are trying to improve.

However, please remember to keep positive and remember that some things just take longer to accomplish than the others.

It is also important to remember that changes in life have different effects. For some people making a change in life is relatively easy, but for some people making a change, even a small change, is difficult. Some people adjust fast, but some people need time. Some people need stability and don't cope with a change very well. However, since changes happen in life, even if we don't want them to, this part of the workbook will hopefully help those who find changes hard to accept.

We all go through changes in life, some are easy to accept, but some are painful. It is up to us what attitude we take towards the changes in our lives, how receptive we are and how open to growth we really are.

When changes in life come unexpected and our life seems to be falling apart, accepting the situation, and understanding the process is a solution half met.

MAKING A CHANGE

Life is constant change and transformation.
Nothing ever stays the same.

Our body is changing with age, our mind adjusting with knowledge, and our soul transforming with experience.

Think about changes in the world that have improved your life for the better.

____

____

____

Resisting change is a painful physical and emotional experience. You can choose to avoid it.

How would your life be today, if those changes would not take place in the world?

____

____

____

____

____

____

____

REJECTION

It is natural to resist change.

We feel comfortable with our life and though we know changes would improve our quality of life, we still refuse to notice the obvious warnings.

Every change in life takes commitment, energy and a **new way of thinking** and behaving.

Sometimes we are just too involved in the illusion of our lives, that we do not see any reasons to change.

What did we gain by changing in the first place?

Do your family or friends keep saying you have an issue or a problem? Though you might not agree with them, what problems/issues do they say you have?

____

____

____

____

____

____

If you think they are wrong, why do you think so?

____

____

____

____

____

____

Is there any truth in what they say? Is there a small possibility that some parts of it is true?

____

____

____

____

____

I know my friends and my family love me and that they want what is best for me.

CONSIDERATION

Birthdays, New Years, Holiday resolutions.
Evening gathering with friends; talking, dreaming, planning...
Another toast to the "new me," another toast to my new life—starting tomorrow!
It's great to think about changes, but let's remember to act on them.

What are the things I always promise myself to do (at resolution times) but never do?

____

____

____

____

____

____

____

What stopped me from acting on my resolutions?

____

____

____

____

____

Change begins in your mind, continues in action, and manifests in your world.

DECISION

Congratulations!

You have made a decision to change.

A decision to change is your goal half reached.

What changes are you implementing in your life?

____

____

____

____

____

How will your life be different?

____

____

____

____

____

When are you starting?

____

Commitment scale 1 - 2 - 3 - 4 - 5 - 6 - 7

Every situation in your life is a result of your decisions and the choices you have made.

What other changes are you implementing in your life?

____

____

____

____

____

How will your life be different?

____

____

____

____

____

When are you starting?

____

Commitment scale 1 - 2 - 3 - 4 - 5 - 6 - 7

I make good choices and
my life is improving because of it.

What further changes are you implementing in your life?

____

____

____

____

____

How will your life be different?

____

____

____

____

____

When are you starting?

____

Commitment scale 1 - 2 - 3 - 4 - 5 - 6 - 7

I feel good about the changes in my life.

ACTION

Your awareness of who you are and what you want from life has lifted you to a new level and you are taking control of your life.

You are acting on your dreams–you are making your dreams come true.

When you are in the action part of your cycle, each action you take, each action you complete, will give you more energy and more motivation.

What am I doing that tells me that I am taking actions in my life? What tells me that I or that my situation is changing? What does my "action life" look like?

____

____

____

____

____

____

____

____

Your life compares to an "action movie"— filled with action, excitement, fun, drama, enjoyment, and the best part is, you get to play the action hero!

You are an action hero!

MAINTENANCE

You need to believe to dream, have courage to take the first step, and have immense energy to commit, but only complete harmony of Body, Mind, and Soul will maintain and sustain your change!

Things and support I need to maintain my change:

____

____

____

____

____

____

Where will I get them?

____

____

Who else I can ask for help and support?

What helped me in past, what works for me that I can re-introduce into my life?

I always move forward and I look back only to see how far I have gotten!

RELAPSE

Some changes in life are not instant.
Some changes in life take time to adjust.
Setbacks are part of the process; setbacks are signs of growth and change.

Do not give up if you relapse.

Keep going!

If you have relapsed, where in the cycle of change will you decide to go now? (Circle)

Rejection Consideration

Decision

Action Maintenance

What is the next step you will take, which will take to the next stage?

____

____

____

When you will take this step? __________________

Commitment scale 1 - 2 - 3 - 4 - 5 - 6 - 7

I relapse for one purpose only: to assure myself that I am on the right path.

Did you always resist change? Remember times in the past that you made changes and you didn't like it.

____

____

____

____

Could you make the changes differently this time?

____

____

____

____

Did you always resist change? Remember times in the past that you made changes and you enjoyed the change; your life was better.

____

____

____

____

What are your main worries about change?
What fear do you associate with change?

____

____

____

____

____

____

____

What about change do you find exciting?
What good feelings do you associate with change?

____

____

____

____

____

____

____

If you find it difficult to change - think:
What will happen if you don't change? How will this affect your life?

____

____

____

____

____

____

____

What will happen if you change?
How will you benefit?

____

____

____

____

____

____

____

What makes me go back to my old habits?

____

____

____

____

____

____

____

My affirmation:

____

____

____

____

What can I do to prevent losing interest?

____

____

____

____

My affirmation;

____

____

____

I know I can only change myself! But there are so many issues that I don't like in others. What are the issues?

____

____

____

____

____

____

OK, I know I can't change others, but what can I do to resolve the issues?

____

____

____

____

____

____

____

My affirmation:

____

____

My plan of action for today:

____

____

I can't change others,
but I can change things which are in my control.

I can change my attitude towards things I cannot change.

When we are no longer able to change a situation,
We are challenged to change ourselves.
- Victor E.Frankl

What will I change about myself?

____

____

Cycle of Change

Where are you in the cycle of change?

This can relate to any topic, issue, or any area of your life. (Circle the appropriate)

I don't have a problem

I am thinking of changing

I have decided to change

I am taking steps to change

I am maintaining my new lifestyle

I have relapsed

I am honest...

On a scale 1 - 2 - 3 - 4 - 5 - 6 - 7

How honest am I?

Steps I will take to keep moving forward and maintaining my cycle of change:

1.

____

2.

____

3.

____

4.

____

5.

____

6.

____

7.

____

Commitment scale 1 - 2 - 3 - 4 - 5 - 6 - 7

When will I take my steps ____________________

In the following area of my life:

____

____

I am in the following part of the cycle of life:

____

____

To continue moving forward I am committing to the following actions:

____

____

____

____

In order to stay in maintenance, I need to focus on the following:

____

____

____

____

In the following area of my life:

____

____

I am in the following part of the cycle of life:

____

____

To continue moving forward I am committing to the following actions:

____

____

____

____

In order to stay in maintenance, I need to focus on the following:

____

____

____

Be the change you wish to see in the world.

-Mahatma Gandhi

In the following area of my life:

____

____

I am in the following part of the cycle of life:

____

____

To continue moving forward I am committing to the following actions:

____

____

____

____

In order to stay in maintenance, I need to focus on the following:

____

____

____

Do not pray for an easy life,
pray for the strength to cope with a difficult one.

Chapter 8

Motivation and Inspiration

We know that goals and dreams are the main motivation and inspiration factors. If our dreams and goals are generated from our heart's desires, they will inspire us to take action, we will be motivated to work hard and we will accomplish whatever we really want.

It is important to keep dreams alive. When working toward our goal we should keep dreaming. We should actually imagining reaching and accomplishing our goals.

Sometimes we get overworked, tired, we come across barriers and obstacles. At times like this we need motivation and confidence the most. Sadly, these are also the times that most people give up on their dreams. So ensure you keep up your motivation and confidence when you are at your lowest point.

If you need to take a short break from everything, then take a break, but do not give up. Always pick up the project where you left it. Do a little bit every day, be consistent. You must know that, without exception, we all face obstacles. The difference is that some people give up, and the others deal with the challenges, and they keep going. This is the only difference.

So be the winner! This part of the life coaching workbook will help you with motivation, so whenever you feel down, work through this part of the workbook; it will help you to stay on your journey. When you commit to your actions and then constantly work toward your goal, you will succeed.

Positive affirmations are great for keeping up motivation. Remember the power of positive thought. When you feel low, all you need to do is change your belief and your thought, keep your mind on your dream, and you will overcome any obstacle in your way.

You are in charge of your thoughts; therefore, you decide how you want to feel. You are in control of your destiny, and you alone will decide if your dream will come true.

So keep dreaming and keep working toward your goal.

Everything is possible!

We are all different; therefore, different people need different motivation and inspiration. What might be motivation for one, would not make a difference for another. This is why this workbook is so great; you will personalize your journal with your own inspirations and motivation.

We don't think about our motivations and our own inspirations, at least not often enough. We just do what others do. We believe that what motivates our friends will also motivate us. Not necessarily. I encourage you to think carefully about your own inspirational and motivational ideas, because only then, they will have a positive effect on your life.

Think about your heroes, people you admire. Their life stories and their courage might inspire you. This section of the workbook will help you toward finding your inspiration and motivation.

I personally keep motivated by daily journalizing, daily meditations and reflections, by keeping positive affirmations on my kitchen cabinets, mirrors, anywhere that I would see them daily. Keep picture of my dream, or picture of me reaching my goal on my mirror or on the fridge. Listening to music, watching inspirational movies, participating in sports.... Reading inspirational and self development books.... There is so much out there to keep you motivated.

I also learned to keep away from people and things that demotivate me! That's an important part.

What motivated you to start this coaching program?

What happened in your life that made you decide on a journey of self-development? What happened in your life that made you decide to implement changes? Did someone encourage you?

____

____

____

____

____

Life gave me a second chance and I took it.

How did you feel when you reached your goals in past?

Can you remember one thing from your past that you could call your success?
You reached your goal. You made it. What was it? It could be something you achieved in school, your first job, anything.

____

____

____

Now remember how you felt when you succeeded. How did you feel in your heart? Just take some time and think about it. Experience your success again.

I can remember my past successes clearly:

____

____

____

____

____

What were others telling me at the time? What do I remember about my success?

____

____

____

____

____

What motivated me in past?

____

____

____

____

What else motivated me? Who motivated me in past?

____

____

____

____

<u>How can I make my journey fun?</u>

You know what your goals are, you know what your action plan is, and you know your possible obstacles.

<u>You are goal oriented.</u>

Remember to keep your journey exciting and fun. Life is not just about reaching your goal, but about enjoying the journey toward your goal.

How can you make your journey more fun?
List anything that comes to your mind.

____

____

____

____

____

____

____

____

____

I have fun because I feel safe – I know what I am doing and I know where I am going.

Keep going

There are many ways to keep motivated and inspired:
Reading self-development books
Relaxing and Meditating
Sports
Using spiritual cards
Reading poetry and inspirational quotes
Watching inspirational Television Programs and Movies
Goal reminder pictures and notes on the walls
Listening or playing music
Goal Maping or collage of your goals

What works for you with regard to motivation and inspiration? What keeps you going?

____

____

____

____

____

____

____

I always ensure my body is comfortable, my mind is tranquil, and my soul is acknowledged.

Constantly revisit your status.

We always need to know where we are.

Most of the time we think we are not doing that well, we think we could do better. We are harsh on ourselves

Keep revisiting your action plan.

You will be surprised how well you are doing.

Celebrate!

I am so pleased with my progress. This week I feel great, I did so well. What was the biggest achievement this week?

____

____

____

____

____

____

I will celebrate by:

____

____

Things you need remove from your life.

It's hard to cleanse and clear away clutter, but we have to. If not all at once, we can declutter step by step. Just adding new things and new activities to our life will clutter our life and it will be harder for us to move on. Unimportant stuff needs to GO.

Don't worry if it takes time to cleanse away events, issues, situations, or even people. Some things need time.

I am taking control of my life. I am changing and moving on. I see things differently and I can now recognize some situations that need to be removed from my life:

1. ____

I will remove them by: ______________________

2. ____

I will remove them by: ______________________

3. ____

I will remove them by: ______________________

4. ____

I will remove them by: ______________________

I am strong.

My plan for decluttering. What will I do. What actions I will take to remove things from my life, things that no longer serve its purpose, or things that stops me from reaching my goals:

____

____

____

____

____

____

____

____

____

____

Who can help me?

____

____

____

____

Commitment Scale 1 - 2 - 3 - 4 - 5 - 6 - 7

Heroes

We are constantly inspired by successful people, their courage and their strength.

Great people make great history.

Can you relate to a particular movie, a book, a character, historic figure or a story?

My inspirations comes from my Heroes:

1.

____

2.

____

3.

____

4.

____

5.

____

6.

____

7.

____

Heroes are ordinary people who make themselves extraordinary. - Gerard Way

What can I learn from my Heroes? How can I implement this in my life?

1.

____

2.

____

3.

____

4.

____

5.

____

6.

____

7.

____

Look closer to home, who withing your family inspires you? What can you learn from them?

____

____

____

We are all the producers of our own plays.
Let's not focus only on dramas...

Motivational Balance

SHORT - term

Positives of staying the same

____

____

____

____

____

____

Negatives of staying the same

____

____

____

____

____

____

Motivational Balance

SHORT - term

Positives of changing

____

____

____

____

____

____

Negatives of changing

____

____

____

____

____

____

Motivational Balance

LONG - term

Positives of staying the same

____

____

____

____

____

____

Negatives of staying the same

____

____

____

____

____

____

Motivational Balance

LONG - term

Positives of changing

____

____

____

____

____

____

Negatives of changing

____

____

____

____

____

____

My own inspirational quotes:

____

____

____

____

____

____

____

____

____

____

____

____

____

____

____

I achieved my goal!

Draw a picture of you achieving your goal or take a photo & magazine picture of your goal. You can draw abstractly, draw whatever your feel. Use colours, pencils...Let your imagination and creation flow.
Express yourself.
Sign and date the picture. Date with the date you plan to achieve your goal.

My Goal Achieved

There is only one success – to be able to spend your life in your own way. -Christopher Morl

Meaning of Life

When I exclude all my material possessions,
what else in life is important to me?

____

____

____

____

Am I paying enough intention to what is important to me?

____

____

____

____

____

If not, what can I do to change things?

____

____

____

____

Soul Searching

What makes me cry?

____

____

____

____

What puts a smile on my face?

____

____

____

____

Feelings that surface after ten minutes of solitude.

____

____

____

____

____

What would my life have to be like for me to say, "I lived my life's purpose"?

____

____

____

____

____

____

____

Do I need to adjust?

____

____

____

____

____

____

____

To find what you seek in the road of life, the best proverb of all is that which says: Leave no stone unturned. –Edward Bulwer Lytton

My Life Purpose:

____

____

____

____

Actions I took:

____

____

____

____

Reaching my dreams made me feel:

____

____

____

____

To climb steep hills requires a slow pace at first.
-Shakespeare

Chapter 9

Coaching Scoring System

To score your commitment, your feelings and your goals are essential. Without a score next to your commitment, you will not know if you really are committed to carrying out your actions or if the goal you have set is really your goal. Scoring is a way of checking and double-checking ourselves.

Scoring is integrated part of the life coaching process.

I have developed my own scoring system that will tell you what you may need to change or address when you score low and where you are in your life coaching process if you score high. My system uses scores from 1 to 7, seven being the highest. I like using the number 7, since it is a divine and powerful number.

The number 7 is regarded as a spiritual number, the number of the God force, or the number of Eternity. Almost all wisdom and spiritual scripts are formed around the number 7. For example: 7 heavens, seven thrones, seven seals, seven churches, seven days, 7 spirits of God, seven angels of the Lord, 7 divas and many more....

But my main connection with number 7 is my scoring system with the 7 chakras of our energy centre and the coaching process that we go through during our self-development.

So, use the scoring system (1–7) to check your commitment, your ideas, your goals, and your actions:

You scored ONE

To make your life coaching session worthwhile and to make your journey of change fun and to ensure you will reach your goals, we should take more time to re-examine your life. Please take your commitment book. Read the following questions and answer them, one by one. Don't go on to the next question until you have answered the previous one. Write down the first thing that comes to your mind.

1. What is your greatest feeling of pleasure?

____

____

2. What would have to happen for you to say, "I have succeeded"?

____

____

3. What is the one thing you wanted to do in life, but you didn't?

____

____

4. What is the one thing you would wish for, if angels would grant you one wish?

____

____

5. What would you like to be remembered as/for?

____

____

6. What are three things that you would do if you were given three months to live: one concerning work, one concerning family, and one concerning you.

____

____

7. What is the one change that you want to see in the world?

____

____

Well done.
Now please take some time to read and re-examine your answers.

These are very powerful questions, and your answers came from your deep subconscious. They hold the key to your happiness, and you should take them into account when making plans and setting yourself goals.

Now you are ready to revisit the section where you scored 1; go through the questions and answers again. How are your answers different this time:

____

____

____

What is your new score?

____

There are four elements: earth, water, air, and fire.
If you scored 1, you are in an element of earth, but missing the rest.

To help you on your journey, you might want to consider the following: read self-development books, attend self-development seminars, continue with your life coaching, join the support groups, or undergo therapy.

You scored TWO

To make your life coaching session work and to introduce new elements into your life, we should take more time and re-examine your life. Please take your commitment book. Carefully consider the following questions and answer them, one by one. Don't go on to the next question until you have answered the previous one. Write down the first thing that comes to your mind.

1. If you lost all your money and positions, what would be the first thing you would do?

____

____

2. Who would you be with, if you had no money?

____

____

3. If you were lost at sea and ended up on an island by yourself, who and what would you miss most?

____

____

4. If you had an unlimited amount of money, but worked only for pleasure, what job would you do?

____

____

5. List seven items/activities that you enjoy doing but don't need money to pay for them.

____

____

6. What are the things in life you cannot do, but wish you could, because you are working too much?

____

____

7. What are the negatives that money brings to your life?

____

____

Well done.
Now please take some time to read and re-evaluate your answers.

These are very powerful questions and your answers came from your deep sub consciousness.

They hold the key to your happiness and you should take them into account when making plans and setting goals.

Do you feel you need to revisit your life coaching session, your plan, you actions, your goals?

Balance in life is important to your well-being and your happiness.

You might also want to ask yourself how big a part do sexuality and sexual pleasures—being sexual—play in your life?

Is your life revolving around money and sexuality? I challenge you to examine your life, your goals, and your actions further.

You might want to consider reading more spiritual books

You scored THREE

You are a very optimistic person. You have a good nature and a good heart. However, you are facing challenges and you are finding the life coaching journey a challenge.

Please ask yourself the following questions:

1. Are the goals really my goals or someone else's goals?

____

____

2. Am I making decisions based on what other people say to me or what other people do?

____

____

3. Am I concerned about what other people think?

____

____

4. Do I look after my own needs?

____

____

5. Do I love myself?

____

____

Have you come to any new understanding about yourself and your life? Are you easily influenced by others? Do you hold on to negative beliefs about you and your abilities to reach goals?

Please take time and go through the questions again.

I challenge you strongly to revisit your topics, your goals, and your action plan.

I am sure that taking into consideration today's findings, your commitment score will be higher next time.

You might consider using positive affirmation, reading self-development books, and continuing with your life coaching program. Meditation and contemplation time is a great way in getting to know yourself.

You scored FOUR

You have created your goals and you have committed to your actions. The energy behind your decisions is flowing through your heart. Most of your decisions are based on your feelings. Your feelings may be positive feelings such as love, compassion, happiness or they may be negative feelings such as anger, jealousy, or lust. It is less likely that you will achieve all your goals and actions, since you have not yet balanced your decisions with your intellect or your mind.

However, if you have set yourself goals and actions, where feelings play a part, you may have a greater chance of success. But, if you want, you can look through your options and actions again, and see how different the outcome would be, should you put more logic into your decisions. Balance your feelings with your intellect.

You might want to consider more physical activity. Also you might want to consider doing things that mentally stimulate you.

Your scored FIVE

You have strong mental power. You have used your intelligence and your logical thinking when making your decisions.

You will achieve your goals, your actions will be accomplished and your tasks completed. You have committed to yourself; you are disciplined. You give yourself your word and your word is a promise that you will accomplish your goals.

However, you have made all your decisions intellectually and logically. You did not take into account your feelings or your values. You are ignoring your spiritual side.

This is all good, but if you start feeling angry about your progress, if you come across barriers, if you don't enjoy the journey or even the goal itself once it is accomplished, you might want to check your plan and balance your life on a mental and spiritual level.

You might want to consider quiet meditation or Yoga

You scored SIX

You used your feelings and your inner power and intuition when making your decision. Your visualization is superb; you can see yourself achieving your goals. What you see in your mind, you will achieve.

Trust your vision. You have the ability to see beyond the material world and you are spiritually aware.

You have made your decisions taking into account your sensitivity and your values. Your life is supported by your empowering beliefs and your values.

Your body, your soul and your mind are balanced and you have made decisions to ensure your life is balanced between your material and your spiritual sides. Therefore your decisions are supported by your higher self and you will achieve your goals.

You might want to consider getting involved in volunteer work

Your scored SEVEN

You have a divine connection and a mystical understanding of life. You have taken the meaning of your life into consideration while making your choices. You know what your purpose in life is and you have made decisions that are wise and at your highest level of consciousness.

You will reach your goals, since they have been set with an understanding of your purpose. You will work through all the barriers life will throw at you, because you have strength, and you will make the right choices and decisions, because you have found the meaning in your life. Your positive attitude is your closest friend. You will enjoy every day of your life.

You will never give up

About the Author

Petra Oblak was born in Slovenia, but has lived in London since 1986.

Petra is a mother of two beautiful children, devoted Life Coach, entrepreneur, author, and philanthropies.

In 1990, Petra graduated as an alternative medicine therapist from ALBO AMI University in Milan, Italy. Her healing energies were measured to be the highest level quantifiable. She has followed in her father's footsteps and become a very successful bioenergy healer. Her family in Slovenia has been practicing healing and herbal medicine for five generations.

Petra's activities in alternative medicine took backstage during her thirty years career in the broadcast industry. She has founded and successfully managed technology companies and successfully launched over 200 Television channels.

In 2008 Petra graduated from The Coaching Academy in England. Petra runs her own Coaching Practise www.bestcoahc.tv and offers both Personal Life Coaching, Business and Corporate & Executive Coaching. In 2009, Petra launched the first Life Coaching TV Channel BeDoHaveTV which broadcasted on Sky and over the Internet, reaching millions of people worldwide.

Petra's main quality as a life coach is her personal experience and her honesty about her life's challenges. Though she is an extremely successful businesswoman in her own right, she has kept her humanity and spirituality throughout her success and believes that people can be successful in business and still have a good, honest, human heart.

Her enthusiasm and love for surfing drove her to spend a generous amount of her time in Hawaii. Surfing and aloha spirit reflect in her life coaching work, especially in her life coaching meditations.

Volunteering and Charity work are integrated part of Petra's life and involved volunteering at COC (London) and Orphanages & Schools in Africa.

This workbook, coaching sessions and coaching workshop are the products of Petra's hard work and commitment in supporting community, organisations and individuals in their journey.

Should you require any support when working through this book, please e-mail me; Petra@BestCoach.TV

If I have the belief that I can do it,
I shall surely acquire the capacity to do it
even if I may not have it at the beginning. -
Gandhi

Made in the USA
Monee, IL
12 January 2024

51644182R00115